Raheem the Referee by Jawad Tariq.

This publication may not be reproduced in whole or in part, or stored in a retrieval system, or transmitted in any form or by any means, electronic, mechanical, photocopying, recording, or otherwise, without the written permission of publisher/author.

ISBN: 978-1-9991106-3-5

Text & illustration copyright ©2023 by Jawad Tariq
Cover design by Dania Zafar
Illustrations created by http://www.rarecreativities.com.
All rights reserved.
Printed in U.S.A./Canada

RAHEEM THE REFEREE

Jawad Tariq

-For referees everywhere

-For Eshaal, my little referee

LET's BEGIN!

TRAVELLING

KICK BALL

JUMP BALL / HELD BALL

Both players are holding onto the ball.

TECHNICAL FOUL

3 POINTS

PUSHING

CHARGING

Foul! You cannot run into the defense when their feet are planted.

HOLDING

DOUBLE DRIBBLING

Violation! You cannot stop or hold the ball with two hands and still dribble.

2 FREE THROWS

Referee

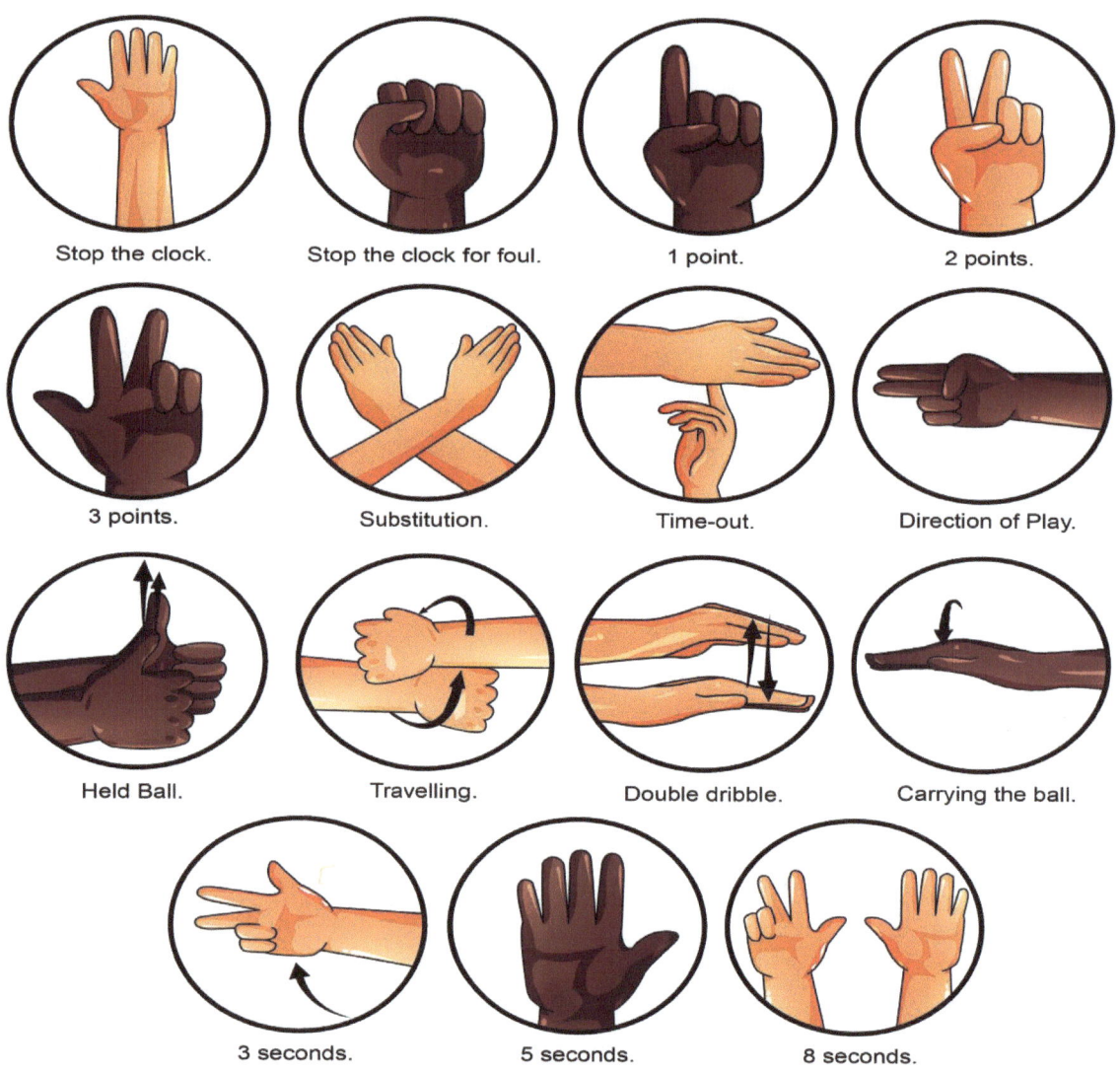

Signals

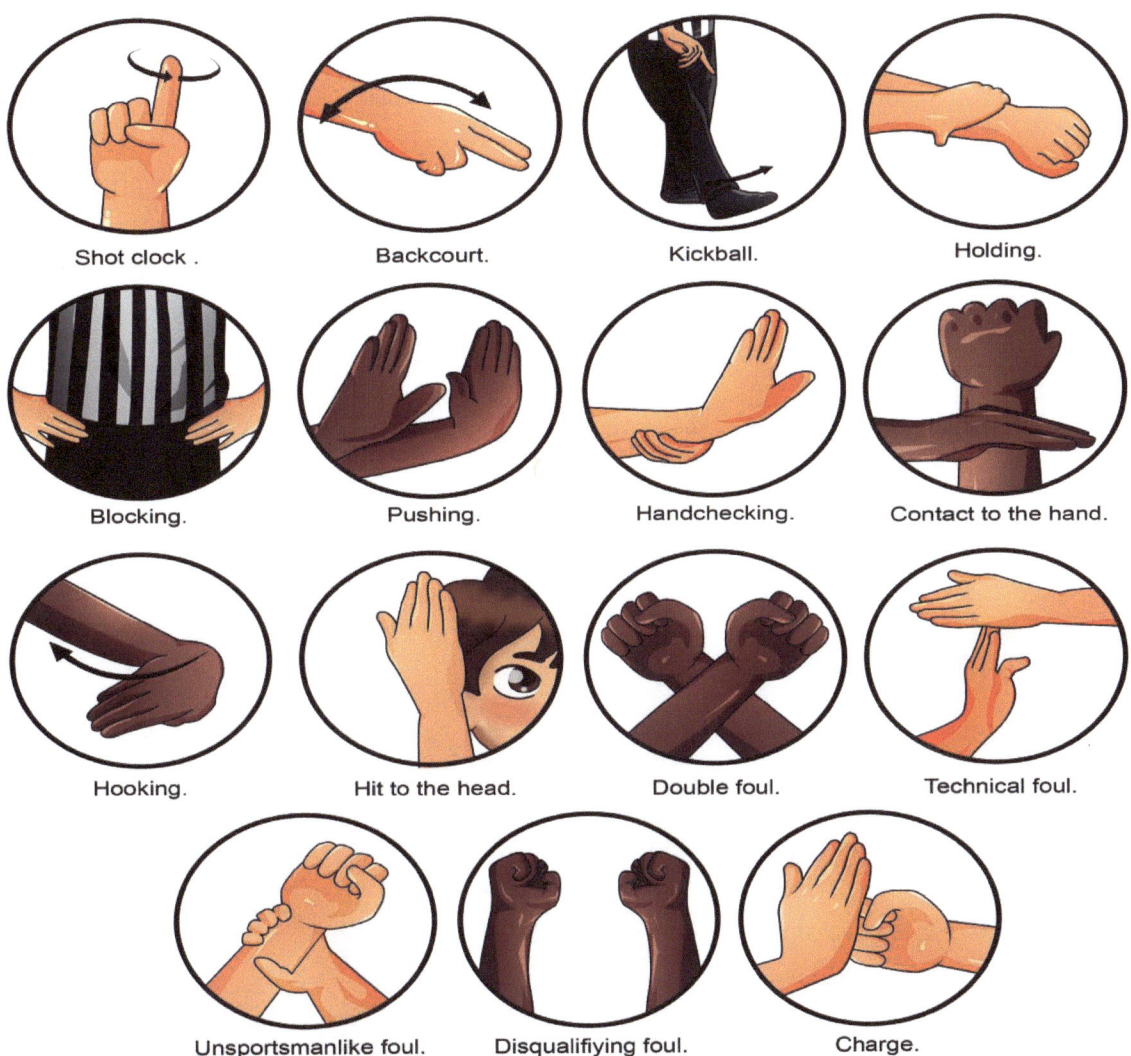

www.ingramcontent.com/pod-product-compliance
Lightning Source LLC
Chambersburg PA
CBHW042051050526
44107CB00109B/1060